THE
SECRET
BOOK
OF
DZYAN

Also by Zinovia Dushkova

The Book of Secret Wisdom

The Teaching of the Heart

Parables from Shambhala

ZINOVIA DUSHKOVA

THE
SECRET
BOOK
OF
DZYAN

**UNVEILING THE HIDDEN TRUTH
ABOUT THE OLDEST MANUSCRIPT IN
THE WORLD AND ITS DIVINE AUTHORS**

Radiant Books

Moscow

Publisher's Cataloging-In-Publication Data

Names: Dushkova, Zinovia.
Title: The secret Book of Dzyan : unveiling the hidden truth about the oldest manuscript in the world and its divine authors / by Zinovia Dushkova.
Description: Moscow : Radiant Books, 2018. | Includes bibliographical references.
Identifiers: ISBN 978-5-6040586-7-1 (paperback) | ISBN 978-5-6040586-8-8 (e-book)
Subjects: LCSH: Theosophy. | BISAC: RELIGION / Theosophy. | BODY, MIND & SPIRIT / Ancient Mysteries & Controversial Knowledge.
Classification: LCC BP561 .D8813 2018 | DDC 299/.934—dc23

British Library Cataloguing-in-Publication Data

A catalogue record for this book is available from the British Library.

Published in 2018 by Radiant Books,
an imprint of Dushkova Publishing, LLC
www.radiantbooks.org

ISBN 978-5-6040586-7-1 (paperback)
ISBN 978-5-6040586-8-8 (e-book)

Dedicated to the 130th anniversary
of the publication of *The Secret Doctrine*
by Helena Blavatsky, whose self-sacrificing
heroic work has ignited the Light of Truth
in our world.

CONTENTS

PART III

THE SECRET BOOK OF DZYAN

INTRODUCTION

In the 19th century, Helena Blavatsky, for the first time in modern history, revealed to the world a few pages from the secret manuscript known as the *Book of Dzyan*, stating that it was created at the dawn of our evolutionary cycle[1] — that is, approximately one million years ago.

Under the guidance of one of the Masters of the Ancient Wisdom, Mahatma Morya, she published in *The Secret Doctrine* two parts entitled *Cosmogenesis* and *Anthropogenesis* that narrated the story of the origin of the Cosmos and humanity. Later, at the beginning of the 20th century, another part under the title *Theogenesis* appeared, which was published by Francia La Due under the guidance of the Master Hilarion.

Nevertheless, all the seekers of Truth still wonder: Is the *Book of Dzyan* real? What is it like? Who are its authors? Where is it and how can one gain access to it?

This and much more will be the focus of our discussion in this publication.

PART I

THE MASTERS OF WISDOM AND THEIR ATTEMPTS TO ENLIGHTEN THE WORLD

The Great Cycle of Cosmic Revelations

In 1824, all the Masters of Wisdom gathered at the Privy Council of Shambhala, which was held in the Ghalaring-Tcho Lamasery near Shigatse in Tibet. One of the main subjects of the Assembly was the question of whether it was worth beginning the great cycle of revealing secret knowledge to humanity — a cycle that would span three centuries and three parts of the world: the West, the East, and the North.

Understanding the unpreparedness of humanity, none of those present expressed much enthusiasm, except for one Master — the Master Morya, who was supported by His Brother Koot Hoomi. Despite all the objections, the Council of Shambhala nevertheless decided to entrust the Mahatmas Morya and Koot Hoomi with conducting this experiment of divulging secret wisdom, unprecedented in the current evolutionary cycle, and with preparing disciples for this task.

Thus, in the 19th, 20th, and 21st centuries, the Master Morya took upon Himself the mission of enlightening humanity through giving the world a cycle of books that, as a whole, compose a certain Teaching, or an integral Triune Doctrine, which would serve as a light-bearing beacon, showing not only the shortest Path from the Mind to the Heart, but also helping people ascend to the heights of Evolution.

And in 2024, the Privy Council of Shambhala will meet again to consider how successful this experiment has been, with a view to making, at the Grand Council of Shambhala in 2025, new decisions based on the available results.

Powers of the Masters of Wisdom

Always, when it comes to the Great Teachers, the question arises: "If the Masters of Wisdom do exist, and They possess those powers that are described so beautifully in works by and about Blavatsky, then why don't They apply Their 'superpowers' to put the world to rights, stop all wars, and establish a long-awaited peace?"

But here we should bear in mind that we do not live in some superhero Hollywood movie, in which all "heroes" can do whatever they want to achieve their goals.

Essentially, the Great Teachers are guests on our planet, who have voluntarily taken responsibility for the evolution of earthly humanity. They have all come from other Worlds, and in various mythologies we can find the confirmation of this fact in the form of legends about the descent of the Gods from the Heavens. And therefore, They are obliged to obey the laws that govern on the Earth, as well as to strictly observe the immutable Laws of the Cosmos.

One of the most important among the latter is the Law of Free Will. It, in turn, requires that the Teachers have no right to violate the free will of people by using supernatural powers and accordingly to intervene in problems created by humanity itself.

The only way They can influence the course of events is either through incarnating Themselves among people or with the help of disciples karmically related to Them, so as to try to bring humanity to reason by "human hands and feet." Of course, when the spiritual biographies of the Teachers and Their disciples become available, we shall see that most of Their incarnations on the Earth with the aim of helping people have ended in a violent death at the hands of Their so-called "brethren" — whether it was crucifixion, burning at the stake, or simply an insidious murder.

However, in the rule of non-intervention in processes on the Earth with the help of supernatural powers, there are two exceptions where the Masters still have the opportunity to intervene at the very last moment, namely:

1. When the life of the entire planet is hanging by a thread because of human activities, but on condition that, in the future, this planet and its humanity will be able to justify such a Sacrifice on the scale of the Universe.

Also, such an intervention is possible with individual disciples sent into the world with a specific mission, when all other opportunities to save them have been exhausted, yet the mission entrusted to them still has not been accomplished, at least minimally. The miraculous healings Blavatsky experienced when she was already close to death are confirmations of this.

2. When humanity itself, either on the whole or within a particular territory, calls upon the Supreme Powers for help and has already applied 50% of the efforts required. But at the same time, the Great Teachers Themselves, if They consider it expedient, can neutralize by half the tragic proportions of various disasters, so to say, as an advance.

Nevertheless, we should not forget that the Great Teachers, or Mahatmas, are not ephemeral Angels soaring in the Heavens, but Human Beings who have attained the supreme level of spiritual development, which in turn determined Their so-called "superhuman" abilities. However, this step cannot be achieved through any mechanical practices, but only through selfless and self-sacrificing service to the world. While all such abilities are destined and present in all people of the Earth, yet they will open in a natural way only when people learn to *love* — as demonstrated by the examples of the Saviours and Saints of all religions.

And although people find it easier to imagine the Great Teachers as Gods, we still need to be alert to a kind of "catch" — to avoid drawing too-perfect images which can eventually lead to excessive idealization.

But when certain pages from the Book of Life of the Masters are revealed to us, and we see that They, while being human, lived like everyone else, and maybe even made the same mistakes that we all did, then it is possible this will result in a sharp rejection of everything that does not fit into the frames of the "ideal picture" created by our own imagination. After all, this is precisely why it is much easier for humanity to revere dead Gods whose idealized image is embodied in sacred scriptures than the living Ones who walk among people and outwardly differ little from them.

The "Centennial Attempt" to Enlighten the World

Before proceeding to our main topic, let us remember the ancient law, which is well-known from the writings of Blavatsky, saying that the Great Teachers should undertake an attempt to enlighten the world once in a century.[2]

For this, the Masters choose a few most worthy people who have been prepared for such a mission over more than one lifetime. They may act both publicly and not publicly, as well as in parallel with each other, being disciples of different Teachers. Through them, the world receives certain Teachings of Light, philosophical systems, scientific discoveries, works of art, literature, and music — everything that is able to help entire humanity expand its consciousness and turn its gaze to the spiritual aspect of life.

However, all those who have studied the works of Blavatsky and become accustomed to the assertion about the "centennial attempt" in *The Mahatma Letters*,[3] have missed one important detail: the Great Teachers do not live according to the calendar of the West. As is well known, They dwell in the heart of the Himalayas, in the kingdom of Shambhala, which is hidden from the external world thanks to secret forces. The Calendar of Shambhala is the Kalachakra Calendar that consists of 60-year cycles, which in turn contain five small cycles of twelve years. This system appeared in India in the second half of the 10th century and was adopted in Tibet in the 11th century, and then spread to other countries in the East, as well as fell into the hands of some Western peoples for sacred calculations.[4]

Therefore, for the Teachers, a "century" consists not of one hundred years, as it may seem at first glance, but sixty. Hundred-year cycles of the Western chronology have significance for the Councils of Shambhala, but only in the context of the sacred number 24, as well as certain dates of the Gregorian calendar when the very numerological code is of importance (such as, for example, the dates of 24 March, 19 July, or 25 December).

Hence all the assertions about "the last quarter of each century,"[5] concerning the Himalayan Masters, symbolically meant precisely the Oriental sexagenary cycle. Indeed, why would Tsongkhapa, the great reformer of Buddhism, remind Tibetan Arhats in the 14th century of this law enjoining them to undertake an attempt to enlighten the world each century,[6] at the same time referring to the Julian calendar (then prevalent in the West) instead of the one under which Tibet lived?

Students, and even more so the disciples who were accepted into the Esoteric Section,* were supposed to comprehend this meaning on their own, after turning the key, and shortly thereafter to welcome the next messenger of the Masters known under the names of Morya and Koot Hoomi — as was forewarned by Blavatsky.[7] In other words, if the years 1875–1890 are considered to be the last quarter of a 60-year cycle, then the next designated period would have been not 1975–2000, but approximately 1935–1950; and further calculations by this formula indicate the period 1995–2010.

The Attempt of the 20th Century

As is known, this promised mid-20th-century disciple who continued the mission of Blavatsky was Helena Roerich; she gave *Agni Yoga* to the world in co-operation with the Master Morya. Through her personal example, she gave "final and irrefutable proofs"[8] of the existence of a secret science — *Gupta-Vidya* — by following the canons and principles of which, she succeeded in mastering the spatial Fire and achieved a supreme state of spirituality on the Earth. In this way, Roerich has left a tool for humanity in the form of the Teaching — a Teaching that allows everyone to master the most powerful elemental force, manifesting itself both in human beings and throughout the Cosmos.

Agni Yoga represents the synthesis of all existing kinds of yoga. And this supreme form of yoga is especially essential today when new fiery energies are incrementally arriving on the Earth from the Cosmos. This is what

* See *Additional Explanations of Helena Blavatsky's Statement about 1975*, p. 51.

people of antiquity warned us about when they predicted the coming of the Epoch of Fire. It is these energies that cause climate change and global warming when virtually every new year breaks temperature records, and the inability of humanity to assimilate these cosmic currents results in natural disasters that have increased manyfold.

Almost every day, from 1920 to 1955, Roerich kept record of conversations with her Teacher that reflected her Fiery Experience — Experience that enabled the Forces of Light to save the planet from imminent death at the end of the 20th century, which was predicted by Edgar Cayce and, besides, Blavatsky herself wrote that the 20th century "may even be the last of its name."[9] The Master determined the period for their publication as "a hundred years" after Roerich's departure, which was reflected in her letters to close colleagues[10] — that is, no earlier than 2055.

Nevertheless, circumstances dictated that in April 2018 — not after a hundred years, but a little more than sixty — the decision was made at the state level to start the full publication of Helena Roerich's records (more than 200 notebooks), which all this time had been kept secret from the public.

Of course, it would be naïve to assume that this happened without the permission of the Masters of Wisdom. Thus, again, it is not the periods of Western chronology that have come into action, but those of the Eastern.

The Main Challenge of the 21st Century

While *Agni Yoga*, echoing ancient sacred scriptures, only warned humanity that "Fire is at the threshold!"[11] it is now already prevalent on our planet. July 2018 alone is enough to mention, with its 118 temperature records around the world![12] Scientists warn that the next five years will also be record hot.[13]

However, unfortunately, the process of global warming will not end in five or fifty or even five hundred years, but will be intensified infinitely with only brief "respites." This is because it does not depend on anthropogenic activity, which indeed brings extreme harm to Nature and people themselves in the first place — and we can only welcome all the initiatives and efforts applied to reduce pollution of the environment. But warming occurs because our whole Solar System is moving in the Cosmos and is now approaching the Central Spiritual Sun — the invisible Source of Fire that is located behind the constellation of Hercules. Indeed, astronomers have already determined that our Sun is moving in the direction of this constellation.[14]

Our planet is not the first and not the last to pass through such a stage in its cosmic evolution, and the rich experience of other systems, which is in the hands of our Teachers, shows that there are only two choices: either assimilation of new fiery energies and adaptation to new conditions, or — explosion. And it is only within the power of the human beings populating a particular planet to make the choice in favour of Life.

Fortunately, thanks to the incredible Sacrifice of the Great Teachers, humanity managed to avoid the explosion of the planet in 1999, not even suspecting how close it stood to the precipice. It was then that our Solar System entered the zone of the increased impact of the currents of the Central Spiritual Sun and other invisible stars and planets. However, as stated in Helena Roerich's notebook recorded in 1953, "the main catastrophe has been postponed for one century — perhaps, even, for two."[15]

After all, if history tends to repeat itself, can we be sure that some variants of the unrealized history that were predicted by such a precise seer as Edgar Cayce, will not be repeated in a different form?

In the matter of predictions, one should always take into account the course of events according to the higher, middle, and lower scenarios. And a prophet can see one of them, which logically leads to a particular phenomenon. But every moment the Cosmic Scales are weighing whether to allow the Karma of either humanity, or a country, or a continent, or a planet to exhaust itself — for example, through an anticipated earthquake, tsunami, epidemic, flood, explosion, etc. — or, thanks to the intervention of the Supreme Powers, to postpone the tragedy, or to turn the course of Time in a different direction. If even trains do not always come on schedule to the minute, what can one say when it comes to the movement of elemental forces on a Cosmic scale?!

The future is always polyvalent, changing every single second. Each of its scenarios is accessible to the gaze of the Great Teachers who stand at the helm of our planet, and They Themselves can affect the future, but only when appropriate. One thing we can say for sure: The Highest Powers will apply every effort to save Planet Earth, but whether the geographical map will be maintained as we know it today, such a question is entirely within the competence of humanity — after all, it is up to humanity to apply at least 50% of the effort required. And so it is far too early for humanity to relax, and if people do not learn how to control the element of Fire that is manifested within themselves in the first place, then it is all the more difficult to predict consequences for individual countries and continents.

And only a pure and loving heart can take on the role of the main transmuter and assimilator of fiery energies — only such a heart is able to tame the element of Fire and to establish people's harmony with Nature. Yet if people are not only unwilling to help their hearts digest these energies — but, on the contrary, burden them even more (as well as the hearts of their neighbours) by their disharmonious thinking and destructive behaviour — then this explains why cardiovascular diseases are now the leading cause of death worldwide, as determined by the World Health Organization.[16] Hearts simply cannot cope with the fiery load and therefore they fail. There are very few hearts on the Earth capable of taking the entire blow of the element of Fire upon themselves in order to protect their areas from upheavals.

It is for this reason that, in the 21st century, all the efforts of the Masters of Wisdom are directed solely at awakening human hearts and providing them with energy assistance. To accomplish this, They have given to the world for use in modern conditions *The Teaching of the Heart — Surya-Vidya*, known to the Initiated from remote antiquity. After all, the more people are able to assimilate the Fire, the more beautiful will be the future of their countries and of the entire planet.

The Cosmic Task of the Entire Solar System

On the whole, the task of the present Solar System, in which we have lived since the beginning of the Sun's origin, is the development of the *heart*. And so all those who descended to the Earth from Distant Worlds bore within themselves the secret knowledge of the significance of the Heart-Sun, which also can be called *Surya-Vidya* in the broadest sense of heartfelt understanding.

And at each stage, a fragment of this knowledge was given so as to first bring to human minds the understanding of how important it is to pay primary attention to the heart.

If we compare all the world religions, all the teachings and philosophies given to humanity by the Supreme Powers, then, despite many seeming differences, we shall still find that Love underlies all of them. And what else expresses Love in us but the heart? So each Teacher of Light has affirmed the omnipotence of a pure and loving heart.

In the same way, Helena Blavatsky, too, provided abundant food in *The Secret Doctrine* for the development of human consciousness, and in this knowledge was laid the wisdom of the principles of Creation. And although at that time the majority of humanity was not yet ready to accept the idea of the supremacy of the heart, she still sowed this thought in the minds of the chosen disciples of the Esoteric Section.[17] Moreover, in her book *The Voice of the Silence*, the Doctrine of the Heart was mentioned as the "Great Sifter"[18] because of the mission which it carries out when it is openly revealed to the world, ceasing to be only for the "elect." Then Helena Roerich brought to the world *Agni Yoga* which expanded humanity's global outlook. It is not by chance that, in the Teaching itself, hints can be found repeatedly that *The Teaching of the Heart* will be given, and the book *Heart* is central in the *Agni Yoga* series.

Indeed, the Path of the Heart can otherwise be called the Golden Path, since, symbolically, gold is the metal of the Sun — the Heart of our planetary system. Servants of Light who lived in ancient times used to divide the cycles of Life into Iron, Bronze, Silver, and Golden Ages, where the latter was the Age of pristine purity, simplicity, and universal happiness — all of which is impossible without a heart wherein Love abides.

However, *The Teaching of the Heart* is not an old manuscript, but represents a reflection of those texts that are recorded on the Fiery Tablets of Eternity, and it is relevant to the Solar System as a whole. *The Teaching of the Heart* is given precisely in current times, when Planet Earth, as well as the entire Solar System, is at a crucial point in its development. The Teaching has taken into account the energy state in which a number of planets both inside and outside of the Solar System find themselves now. This also includes the living beings that dwell on them, even though they are inaccessible to our physical vision.

The Influence of Cosmic Currents on People

Studies from the *Voyager* spacecraft now show that "tsunami waves" take place in the Solar System[19] which simply cannot but affect our planet as well. We live in an absolutely unique time when humanity, under the influence of the currents of the Central Spiritual Sun and other visible and invisible stars, is changing at the cellular level.

In April 2018, Australian scientists were able for the first time to detect a mechanism through which this might happen — namely, a new DNA structure that was not previously observed in living cells, but studied in the laboratory. This structure, called an *i-motif*, appears and disappears, depending on environmental conditions. Scientists assume that this i-motif helps the body control "turning on" and "turning off" certain genes, launching or stopping certain processes.[20]

From what has already been revealed by the Great Teachers, it is known that people need not grow old and die. Instead, they may simply flow from one form into another with the help of alchemical processes occurring at the cellular level. However, for this, two conditions must be observed:

1. The energy environment must favour a change in human structure. We are currently living in just such a time.

2. People and their hearts must be prepared for this; otherwise no changes will happen, or those that do occur will bring undesirable consequences. Unfortunately, only one-sixth of the world's population is potentially ready for this.

Nevertheless, already now it may be assumed that, under the influence of cosmic currents, the above-mentioned mechanism in our cells will enable the best part of the present population to form a completely new evolutionary type of humanity — one that will live on the Earth in future centuries, just as the secret *Book of Dzyan* tells us.

However, as was already said, the perception of these currents is associated with risk and danger, not only for people, but also for countries, continents, and the planet as a whole. It is dangerous because such currents have never reached the Earth before. Fortunately, at the level of the Human Kingdom, there are always pioneers who must undergo everything themselves, who voluntarily agree to participate in the Fiery Experiment and thereby help the Masters of Wisdom find the necessary formulas of Rays to saturate space with.

And what happens here? When a powerful influx of energy comes from the Cosmos, people with disharmonious thinking and behaviour (or those surrounded by such individuals) are unable to pass this energy through their hearts properly — while circulating through certain channels, it may settle on one of levels. Then a rapid growth of cells begins because the new energy has settled there. After some period of time, they may themselves dissolve or disappear as an outflow of energy; in other cases, the modified cell may grow, for example, into a benign or malignant tumour. That is why statistics show an increase in various types of cancer, and the World Health Organization predicts that the number of cancer cases will rise in the next 20 years by 70%.[21] In this case, it is the hardest for the heart, since it occupies a border position between the lower and the higher structure of the human being.

Some people are specifically born to be present at the junction of epochs when new currents come, and they voluntarily take this blow upon themselves. And these people may take on quite consciously the karma of others, their beloved ones or relatives, their nation or country. They in no way deserve such serious diseases, but accept them consciously or subconsciously to help others.

Different moments may be found on physical, emotional, and mental levels. Everything is monitored by the Great Teachers — after all, They need to discover new formulas so that illnesses will no longer appear on any of the levels. Yet this requires time.

Ancient prophecies said that, at the end of time, nine out of every ten people would be insane. At a certain stage in the development of a human being, which is also applicable to all of humanity, there is a test called *adequacy*. Today there is a lot of insanity in the world, which can emerge on the level of mental bodies, as well as penetrate the astral, emotional, and mental bodies from the so-called "erring mind."

Diseases at the level of mental bodies are the most dangerous because they can lead to the annihilation of the entire planet. Indeed, such "malignant illnesses" open the door to obsessions — a chance that is never missed by anti-evolutionary forces. So we all hear on the news of increasing incidences of sudden shootings and attacks in schools and crowds around the world, even in supposedly calm countries where such things have never happened before. Also, diseases and epidemics at the level of mental bodies can result in mass disorders with the use of poisonous chemicals, in the creation of different types of weapons of mass destruction for bloodshed and fratricidal wars, as well as in other negative things.

Colleagues of the Brotherhood are composing new combinations of Rays, which are already being projected into the world with the aim of healing the greater part of humanity. And here the main focus of fires is the heart, which alone is capable of accepting and assimilating currents of the highest frequency. Thus, a loving heart is able to heal any illness, provided it is open to the Rays of salvation, which are pouring forth from secret laboratories controlled by the Hierarchy of Light.

Of course, just as in all previous centuries, it is up to humanity to accept or reject the help now being offered by the Highest Powers. However, in the latter case, people should be aware of what consequences await them and not complain of being abandoned by the Supreme Powers, after repeatedly rejecting Their outstretched Hand.

"Hitherto Shalt Thou Go, and No Further"

So says another rule that determines for the disciples of the Great Teachers that no divulgence of secret knowledge, including the description of sacred manuscripts, can happen, unless They have made an appropriate decision. And such a decision must be based on the cosmic and spatial conditions, as well as on the overall preparedness of humanity and a multitude of other factors that are difficult to embrace by the earthly mind.

For many readers who are familiar with the works of the disciples of the Great Teachers, such as Helena Blavatsky and Helena Roerich, as well as with *The Mahatma Letters*, the dependence of publication of certain information on periods will not be surprising at all. However, to those who are unacquainted with this fact, we shall give two examples for illustration.

During the preparation and publication of *Isis Unveiled* in 1877, Helena Blavatsky still could not speak openly about the sevenfold structure of human beings and the planet, leaving only hints. However, already in *The Secret Doctrine*, published in 1888, she gave this information with all clarity — which caused attacks on the part of critics who accused her of contradicting herself. So we see that disciples inviolably observe this rule, even to the detriment of their own reputations.

Further, on the one hand, Blavatsky used the conventional calculations of Kali Yuga (the Dark Age), which was to end only in an unimaginably enormous number of years. On the other hand, she left a hint that many of her contemporaries would witness a New Cycle,[22] and she repeatedly stated that the cited calculations for the duration of epochs were merely symbols, while the real keys belonged to the Initiates alone.[23]

Knowing the actual period for the end of Kali Yuga and the beginning of Satya Yuga (the Light Age identical with the Age of Aquarius) — 1942 — Helena Blavatsky still kept it in secret and used only the information which was available to all. Only in the late 1930s, when researchers themselves were able to understand that the gigantic figures indicated were simply symbols and widely informed the population of India about this, did the Great Teachers confirm — through Helena Roerich — the accuracy of those calculations. At the same time, it is known from Roerich's notebooks that she was aware of this date from the Master Morya even earlier.[24] And on 1 August 1943, the cosmic event occurred that was described in the *Vishnu Purana* (Book IV, Chapter XXIV) as the sign of Satya Yuga's beginning, which Blavatsky cited in *The Secret Doctrine*.[25]

Many may not agree that the Light Age began in 1942, while only one day earlier it was the Dark Age. Of course, gigantic cataclysms still occur in the form of earthquakes, volcanic eruptions, and tsunamis; in addition, wars are waged, blood is shed, and innocent children die. And, nevertheless, even after a doctor removes a malignant growth, one still can have bleeding wounds and experience pain for a long time. However, life already triumphs in one's body — life that has conquered the death which threatened one.

Similarly, a spring that arrives on 1 March may be accompanied by huge snowdrifts, though it is only a matter of time before last year's snows melt. Yet the Sun is already shining in a new way! And most importantly, we should always remember that the Calendar of Shambhala is not based on phenomena obvious to the human gaze, but on those mysterious processes which occur at the level of the Subtle Plane's phenomena. It is only a matter of time before the Secret is revealed.

Thus, up until just a few years ago, in 2015, when the new stanzas of *Agapegenesis* were published in *The Book of Secret Wisdom*, it was possible to say about the *Book of Dzyan* only what was known from the writings of Helena

Blavatsky. However, now that humanity has passed the most decisive period in its evolution — the year 2017 — it has become possible to unveil entirely new information about this mysterious manuscript.

PART II

THE HIDDEN DEPOSITORIES

OF THE SACRED WISDOM

OF THE AGES

An Ancient Legend

Many centuries before Helena Blavatsky, in the pre-Christian times of Kievan Rus, there were legends that have descended to our days concerning the existence of the Great Book known as the *Book of Doves*. There are more than twenty versions of legends about it, many of which were altered to fit the Christian worldview. The prominent Russian artist Nicholas Roerich, who is known to have had access to the same sources as Blavatsky, even created two paintings dedicated to the legend of the *Book of Doves*.

According to tradition, this Book fell from the Heavens on the White Mountain to the burning Alatyr Stone on the White Island of Buyan, which is "destined to rest amidst the bottomless ocean ever since the beginning of time."[26] It was written in the language of the birds by one of the Supreme Gods of the Slavic mythology, who later became associated with Christ. Hence the Book's name, which could also mean "profound" or "wise" in the Old Slavic language.

Legend has it that many kings from all over the world came to see it, but no one could read it. And those few people who could, "read the Book for exactly three years and read exactly three pages."[27] In every myth, the *Book of Doves* is called the Mother of all books, for "the entire Wisdom of the World is concealed in it,"[28] and it contains knowledge about the origin of the world and humanity.

The brief information of this ancient legend already provides answers to the basic questions concerning the *Book of Dzyan*:

- It has an extra-terrestrial origin and was brought to the Earth from Distant Worlds by the Great Teachers.

- It is connected with the magical stone of mythologies of many peoples around the world — the Chintamani Stone, which was also brought by the Great Teachers as a Gift of Orion.
- It is preserved on the White Island — that is, in Shambhala which, according to *The Secret Doctrine*, is the only continent destined to last from the beginning to the end of the Grand Cycle of Evolution.[29]
- It is written in *Senzar*, a universal language of all Creation, which is often referred to as the language of the birds or angelic language in the mythology of various peoples of the world.
- Just a single page of the Book contains a mass of information, but only if one who has gained admittance to it has the ability to read.

Secret Depositories

The Teachers of humanity, our Elder Brothers and Sisters, store in their Depositories only the best pages composed over the entire history of the Earth's evolution. In addition, Truths that were brought from Distant Worlds and are available only at certain levels of Initiation, are sacredly preserved.

Some Earth-dwellers have been granted the right to be guided by the Teachers of humanity. And at certain stages of discipleship, secret pages related to the Laws governing the Universe were revealed to them. And not only their own destiny, but that of all humanity depended on what use they made of this knowledge.

Such Depositories are located virtually all over the world, in the depths of mountain ranges and beneath the sands of vast deserts of different countries and continents. Many people wonder why, if all this really exists, the Teachers Themselves do not open them and make everything available to the public?

By way of reply, it is enough to ponder such questions as: For what purpose and in what domains are the most advanced technologies used — directly they are discovered and developed by scientists? Is this medicine along with education or military industry with all the consequences that come with it?

Unfortunately, the answer is obvious. Even today we can see how certain personalities in pursuit of profit stop at nothing: they are all too prone to cutting down forests, polluting the purest waters, and poisoning the air and thereby people — not to mention the fact that human lives, too, often have no value for them. And what would happen if this secret knowledge fell into the hands of such people? What they would do to the planet then?

After all, knowledge is knowledge: it itself is neither good nor evil. However, if it becomes available to all, then how can we control what hands will get at it and in what way it will be used? Indeed, it is human hands that add either a light or a dark coloration to knowledge.

For example, Edgar Cayce said that under the paws of the Sphinx there was a secret entrance leading to the "Hall of Records" of Atlantis.[30] The research of various scientists using radar and seismological methods at the end of the 20th century demonstrated that there are indeed a cavity and tunnels.[31] However, further research was suddenly forbidden and now the Egyptian government officially prohibits conducting any kind of research around the Sphinx. Obviously, this prohibition is not accidental, and the deciding vote is certainly not cast by the government of Egypt, but by the Masters of Wisdom, who should first notice a confident change in the world's balance of powers in favour of Good.

Therefore, all Depositories across the globe are under the protection of mysterious powers until humanity learns to use the obtained secret knowledge for the benefit of all, and this is possible only with the proper development of the qualities of the *heart*. All the more so since the Earth has already experienced the march of heartless humanity of the previous cycle which, with the highest knowledge at its disposal, exterminated itself to such an extent that virtually no trace is left.

And so, for the sake of the people who are not yet ready for such knowledge, none of the passers-by can get access to these Depositories, even when such a treasury is situated right under their feet.

Is There Any Evidence?

Some might say: "Bring us real evidence of the existence of the Masters and the *Book of Dzyan*, and then we'll believe you."

But often the problem with human nature is that those who demand proofs really want to convince themselves and others of the non-existence of a certain phenomenon. And therefore, no matter what "real" evidence is provided, they will demand something even "more real"; in the end, they will announce that everything provided them to date is fake, just so they can stay with their negation, and will go so far as to call the provider a charlatan or fraud. Is not this what happened to Helena Blavatsky, who, instead of devoting her time and energy to writing the third, fourth, and fifth volumes of *The Secret Doctrine*, wasted them in constant attempts to respond to all the accusations of "scientific society"?

Yes, for many people it is still easier to simply deny everything than to accept Truth as it is. Of course, no one

will bring the *Book of Dzyan* out of Shambhala only to
convince someone of its existence. In such cases, one is
reminded of the parable of the disciple who came to a
Teacher and said: "Show me a miracle, and I'll believe in
you and your Teaching." With a sad smile, the Teacher
showed him a miracle, whereupon the disciple joyfully
exclaimed: "Now I'm ready to follow you!" The Teacher
replied, however: "But now I no longer need you."

The Great Teachers do not need disciples who demand miracles and proofs. They already made an excep-
tion to the rule and demonstrated miraculous phenomena
with the help of Blavatsky. However, no one who was at-
tracted in this way, unfortunately, lived up to Their expec-
tations, and none of them has ever become a true disciple.
Still, the Masters were targeted with so many accusations
during that short period that their repercussions lasting
for ages to come.

By the way, until now, none of her critics has ever
explained how Blavatsky managed to "forge" everything.
Yet a hundred years after her death, her accusers nevertheless admitted[32] that all charges against her had been based
on forged evidence; moreover, those who forged it made
no attempt to hide the fact that they had done this for
money offered by missionaries.[33] Unfortunately, killing
first and then justifying has become a "good tradition" in
the history of humanity.

Indeed, a multitude of proofs has already been found,
testifying to the existence of ancient civilizations which
preceded ours, such as Lemuria and Atlantis. However,
"official science" up to the present day prefers to "reward"
all inquisitive researchers in different fields of activity
with the prefix *pseudo*: pseudoscientist, pseudohistorian,
and so on. And where the authenticity of the evidence is
beyond a shadow of a doubt, then such facts are simply

suppressed or discredited by all possible means — after all, they do not fit into the framework of the worldview invented by the "official" history, which believes that reasonable humanity has been living on the Earth for a mere 300 thousand years or so and absolutely ignores the cyclicity of evolution. Of course, to someone with such a lack of understanding, the very assumption that somewhere there exists a million-year-old manuscript seems to be completely absurd.

Here we can also recall the relatively recent example of the apocryphal Tibetan Gospel entitled *The Life of Saint Issa, the Best of the Sons of Men*. Nicolas Notovitch revealed its translation for the very first time to the peoples of the West. Yet, during his lifetime, he was discredited in every possible way, so that the truth about the years Jesus Christ spent in the countries of the East would not become commonly known. Later, the authenticity of this text was confirmed by Nicholas Roerich[34] and Swami Abhedananda.[35] But, for some reason, to all other researchers, monks reply that they have never heard of that manuscript.

The thing is that Buddhist monks, the guardians of ancient manuscripts, have a well-developed intuition and they will never confirm its existence — and especially will not show it — to unworthy people, even at the cost of their own lives. In some monasteries there are secret sacred treasuries that are accessible solely to lamas of an exceptionally high spiritual level. These repositories are sometimes called "black," because they are usually dug in the bowels of the earth, and sacred objects are kept there without daylight, maintaining a special temperature and energy components that are composed by uttering special mantras. But ordinary monks, of course, know nothing about these treasuries.

In the same way, the original of the above-mentioned Tibetan Gospel is stored in a secret room. However, only very few have been honoured to behold the copy of the manuscript in the language of Pali — among them a certain Englishman, whose name cannot yet be disclosed. As a rule, one who has been admitted into such a Holy of Holies must not reveal more than the guardians of ancient apocrypha permit.

The Tower of Chung

The Chief Depository is located in the Tower of Chung in Shambhala, the legendary City of Gods, also known as the White Island. There are so-called "outposts" in the form of small ashrams or hidden caves, which are directly connected with Shambhala, and they form a special protective net which no one can pass through unless they are invited. So Helena Blavatsky was called in the 19th century and Helena and Nicholas Roerich in the 20th.

The Tower of Chung, where the Great Lord of Shambhala is on eternal watch, is a multi-storey structure which goes deep into the Earth as well as rises high above into the Subtle Spheres. It may be called a gigantic museum, where all the works of art of all peoples and continents that have ever existed on our planet are stored. There is a large library of numerous manuscripts and literary works of all time, including those that have been considered lost or destroyed long ago.

After all, there have been so many wars in human history and so many libraries with the most beautiful books that have been simply destroyed. However, Messengers of Light still managed to save and copy many of them — even at the cost of their own lives — and to bring them all into the Library of the Tower of Chung.

These dilapidated manuscripts, written in all the languages that have ever existed on the Earth, are stored in special conditions, because it is important to preserve the energy of the epochs when they were created from the materials available to humanity of a certain time-period. Of course, the Teachers have their copies created from a special composition of matter that is characteristic of secret manuscripts, such as the *Book of Dzyan*.

The Tower of Chung also contains absolutely all the exhibits of the Mineral, Vegetable, and Animal, as well as Human Kingdoms — in short, all the patterns of Life that have ever existed on the Earth in the form of subterranean or terrestrial inhabitants. They are immersed in centuries-old dormancy in special niches which are filled with certain gaseous substances to preserve life at the cellular level.

An Abandoned Ancient Tower

As the secret notebooks of Helena Roerich have already been made public, it is now possible to say that the Tower of Chung had been situated in the mountains of Tian Shan since post-Atlantis times up until the middle of the 20th century.[36] However, the location of Shambhala is interconnected with the core of the Earth and the Fiery-White Core of the Sun, and therefore it may be movable. This, as well as changes in the earthly atmosphere caused by the world wars, has forced the Teachers to move the Tower of Chung to a new place in the Himalayas.

In the conversations recorded in Helena Roerich's notebooks, Mahatma Morya told her that one pilot

PART II

had dropped a bomb into the valley where the Masters lived. This caused a change in the atmosphere, making it unbearable for Them, and also destroyed records and broke one extremely delicate device used in conducting research.[37] And here a question may arise: If a dropped bomb could change the atmosphere and destroy the records of the Teachers, then to what extent is Shambhala protected by mystical powers?

But the fact is that the Teachers were preparing to move to a new dwelling place even before that incident. The Abodes where the Lords work are abandoned with the expiry of a certain period and turned over to free public access. Such places exist in Shigatse and Darjeeling. There are also devices used for work under earthly conditions, but they are constantly evolving, so if something happens to them, there is no great tragedy in this, as they have already accomplished the main task entrusted to them. Of course, they could be placed in the Tower of Chung as museum pieces. But who will now yearn for pagers when mobile phones are commonplace?

Shambhala is invulnerable, yet there are a number of Abodes of the same name which are connected with it. If a branch is cut off a tree, the roots will still continue to live and the trunk will reproduce a new branch. Of course, manuscripts can also be restored from the Chronicles of Akasha, but only if there is a supreme expediency for this — when energy expenditures for their complete restoration are justified.

As regards the former Tower of Chung, as Mahatma Morya said, it was abandoned, standing empty now as a proof of the Masters of Wisdom's existence in the mountains of Tian Shan, along with some of Their devices and numerous manuscripts in Sanskrit-like languages unknown to modern science.[38] When humanity is ready,

31

the destined person or group of researchers will discover all this, as recently happened with the Dead Sea Scrolls.

Access to Secret Knowledge and Its Disclosure

Thanks to their Masters, disciples gain access to the knowledge preserved in the scrolls collected in the Library of the White Brotherhood; such knowledge comprises several levels, like a pyramid. At each level of ascent, disciples do have the right to receive certain knowledge, but first they must take a vow of silence — they must swear to keep any received knowledge secret until special cosmic and spatial conditions come about or until the Council of Lords decides to open yet another page revealing the Mysteries of the Cosmos to the world.

When such a decision is made, a certain Master assumes the responsibility of preparing one of His disciples — the one who is most suitable for the assigned mission. The disciple's subtle bodies, in addition to his previous accumulations, are infused with certain sacred Knowledge even before his birth. And further, before he starts recording the destined works, his Chalice is also systematically filled with qualitatively new currents, accompanying the inflow of new Truths. After all, the Cosmos is renewing itself every moment through the creation of new combinations of Universal Fires. It should also be noted that the Master works with the disciple through dreams as well, although the disciple may not remember this.

Disciples who have successfully completed a cycle of their incarnations and who are in the physical world, so to speak, for the last time, are entitled to share their accumulated knowledge, experience, and so on. As a human being, soul, and spirit, they bring to light works that are written with the Blessing of Fiery Hierarchs who patronize a particular country or an individual people, taking into account the vibrational sound of the currents required at a certain time on specific soils.

In addition, those who arrive from other star systems, Demiurges-Builders and Planetary Spirits, as well as Their disciples, can bestow a cycle of other works as a Gift upon our planet, so as to share the knowledge and experience accumulated in their own Worlds. Such works have a cosmic and spatial significance, but much of what is expounded in them may not relate directly to the Earth in the period of its formation in the 19th–21st centuries.

Of course, history knows sad cases of disciples betraying their Masters. By tradition, disciples who have achieved the level of Earthly Master renounce their own names and not only adopt the Names of their Masters, but begin to act on Their behalf. However, some disciples, after gaining access to the first levels of Knowledge about Cosmogony, have failed to pass yet another test and turned away from the Forces of Light — like Lucifer, who millions of years ago betrayed the Great Teachers and afterwards became identified with the devil.

These disciples thus broke the vow of silence, and attempted to sow prematurely in unprepared soil, divulging without the permission of the Great Teachers the secret knowledge which they had managed to receive from Them. Often such sharing was not carried out through the specific Ray through whose fires certain Knowledge was destined to be transmitted. This resulted in a great number of distortions and terrible consequences at the level of the mental bodies of those people who imbibed that energetically distorted knowledge. And, accordingly, these situations cast a shadow on the lives of the earthly colleagues of such treacherous disciples.

Hence, only the Council of Lords decides when, who, and under what circumstances to reveal certain pages of the *Book of Dzyan*. Besides the Masters, it can also be accessed personally by Their disciples who have passed the Initiations of high degrees.

PART III

THE SECRET

BOOK OF DZYAN

Conditions for the Preservation
of Sacred Manuscripts

The *Book of Dzyan* is stored among other archaic manuscripts on one of the floors of the Tower of Chung. For each of the priceless artefacts a special niche was created which was imbued with the currents of those times when a given manuscript first came to light. Further, the energy constant of the currents is preserved, thanks to a specially constructed covering — a "vitreous" substance, which has a clearly defined geometrical shape. Thus the manuscripts bear within themselves an extremely powerful energy potential for many millennia to come.

Similarly, the volumes of the *Book of Dzyan* are preserved, and although they who gain access to them are able to behold them with their own eyes, nevertheless, the volumes must remain in their energy niches, and should not be touched by human hands. The needed pages will open all by themselves, simply from a touch on the Subtle Plane by the Master who invited one of His disciples to look at them, after first receiving permission for this from the Great Lord of Shambhala.

Titles of Ancient Books

If any of the most ancient books is mentioned by the Teachers in the Human Kingdom, its title appears either orally or in writing. However, when conversing with each other, the Teachers do not use names that are typical of human speech. The true titles of the manuscripts are kept secret, and represent particular constants of light, as well as colour "sound."

Hence the very word *Dzyan* meaning "Secret Wisdom" in Tibetan is merely the generic name given to us to designate this sacred manuscript and its volumes.

The *Book of Dzyan* and Other Legendary Artefacts

Many have learnt about the mystical Chintamani Stone, a fragment of which "travels" around the world, passed from hand to hand by those chosen by the Supreme Forces to accomplish a certain mission for the good of Evolution. The last time it belonged to the Roerich family. And then there is the Holy Grail — how many hunters have searched for it!

While much is still hidden from human eyes, all artefacts collectively form a single "family," linked by energy bonds, which are a lot stronger than blood ties. On occasion they act separately, even while maintaining their indissoluble links. And this connection represents multistage levels of energy sound — starting from relatively material ones that operate in three-dimensional measurement, up to those that are utterly inaccessible to the understanding of the human mind, for they bear within themselves a minimum twelve-dimensional sound.

Thus, since we cannot view the *Book of Dzyan* in isolation from other artefacts, we are yet unable to set forth its full profile. And this will become possible only when the time comes for humanity to learn the truth about the already known legendary artefacts as well as those that are still unfamiliar even to the most accepted disciples of the Hierarchy of Light — disciples who are at the very first stages of comprehending the Great Secrets of the Cosmos.

The Composition of the *Book of Dzyan*'s Pages

The *Book of Dzyan* consists of a special "materialized substance" that outwardly resembles "palm leaves"[39] — a term often used in its description to facilitate a better understanding on the part of those who have turned their gaze towards the comprehension of what this sacral Book represents.

The Teachers of humanity who came from Distant Worlds brought gifts to the Earth in the form of stones, birds, animals, plants, and so on. But not all seeds germinated here, and some of those that sprouted have mutated. There are also those that have left the stage of Life after completing their segment of Evolution.

Thus, in addition to energy components, the matrix structure of the *Book of Dzyan* is also formed from the semi-rarefied substances of certain plants which are unknown to modern science. The transient state from a crumbling stone to a plant forming thin threads inside itself, similar to the germs of roots, can be found in different parts of the world.

Such an unusual composition of matter has enabled the Masters to create voluminous but, at the same time, amazingly light books that cannot be affected by either fire or water or air.

The Structure of the *Book of Dzyan*

And so, what can we say about this "materialized substance" of the *Book of Dzyan*? In its matrix structure, it contains energy constants which are intrinsic to the sound of the core of Sirius, but maximally attuned to vibrations inherent in the planet Earth.

As human beings possess a "physical" quaternary and a spiritual triad, so the Book in the given context has a "material" septenary and a spiritual quinary. Here on the Earth we can talk only about pages accessible to physical vision — which, however, could be more accurately termed spiritual vision, or the vision of the heart.

The spiritual quinary of the *Book of Dzyan*, or its main volumes, which Blavatsky mentioned in draft versions of her articles as "secret folios of *Kiu-te*,"[40] are accessible only to the Teacher of Teachers, as well as the Teachers Themselves. The Wisdom of the World contained in them concerns not only our Earth and humanity, but also the entire Solar System and constellations associated with it. However, these volumes cannot be described in any way, and their age is even impossible to imagine.

Through the reflection of reflections, this most secret part of the *Book of Dzyan* that conceals the synthesis of everything has been partially "deposited" in the Ethereal layer as an intermediary link. This kind of introduction to knowledge in the domain of the Unknown is intended primarily for study by those individuals who no longer have the status of disciples, but have achieved the level of a Teacher of the Earth.

At the same time, the volumes of its "material" septenary, which are available to the disciples of high degrees of Initiation, may be viewed as Commentaries on the above-mentioned secret folios. These Commentaries are created by the Masters with each new evolutionary cycle, and they perform the role of the *Book of Dzyan* for the appropriate stage of development.

The *Book of Dzyan* and Human Evolution

As is known, each of the seven stages of evolution (termed *Races* in esoteric philosophy) through which all humanity is to pass, implies the maximum development of one of the seven principles (or bodies) of a human being in a given Round. Every new cycle in its main features repeats the previous one before advancing humanity to a new level.

For the most part, we now represent the Fifth Race, whose task is to develop *manas*, or the highest mind. So we must have already traversed the repetition of the stage of developing the lowest mind, or intellect, typical of the Fourth Race (the Atlanteans whose high intelligence brought them to a dead end and self-destruction) and are now moving to the spiritual consciousness contained in the heart. And the task of the Sixth and Seventh Races will now be the development of the principles of *buddhi* and *atma*, or soul and spirit, respectively — that is, their evolution will also lay the main emphasis on the development of the heart as the most important organ in the human being — representing the supreme triad of *manas*, *buddhi*, and *atma*.

Thus, as already mentioned, before the beginning of a new cycle, the Teachers create a new volume of the "material" septenary of the unified *Book of Dzyan* for the purposes of those evolutionary tasks that a new Race is destined to accomplish. It is then from that manuscript that all other exoteric and esoteric commentaries and sacred texts for the humanity of the given cycle are derived. This all should provide the maximum and all-round help to people to achieve the necessary development before their transition to the next cycle.

By analogy with the evolution of humanity, we can say that each new volume of the *Book of Dzyan* repeats the same ideas — or rather, is based on what was expounded in the previous one — but proceeds further in its narrative. Setting forth secret knowledge in a new dominant Ray, these volumes reveal ever new facets of the One Truth that will serve for creating new sciences and philosophies at the specified period of time. But we must add that all the derivative texts are also created in certain Rays, at the same time preserving in themselves the dominant note of the Ray in which the main volume was written.

Volumes of the *Book of Dzyan* for Present and Future Times

From the above description it follows that the excerpts revealed by Helena Blavatsky in *The Secret Doctrine* came from one volume of the *Book of Dzyan* intended for the Fifth Race, and therefore, as she said, its narrative did not extend further than the beginning of Kali Yuga.[41]

This folio was written by the Masters approximately one million years ago, when the Atlanteans still existed, although their main continent had already been destroyed, while Shambhala was an island in the ocean. This manuscript is indeed the oldest book and the source of all religions, philosophies, and sciences — but only in the context of the current cycle, and so it may be viewed as one of the volumes of Commentaries on the secret folios of the *Book of Dzyan* — or *Kiu-te*. Of course, there are even more ancient volumes of the *Book of Dzyan* and all the texts originating from them that belong to the times of the previous Races.

Hence, now that the first representatives of the Sixth and Seventh Races have already appeared in the world, it is not difficult to understand that, shortly before the present times, the Masters created a new volume of the *Book of Dzyan* designed specifically for humanity of the future, whose task will be the complete opening of the heart's potential. And so this new volume is expounded in the Ray of Love-Wisdom, which contributes to the awakening of the heart, and its pages embrace the times of the past, present, and future Races, symbolically stopping at the beginning of a New Round of Evolution.

Of course, in the future, it is precisely this folio that will be the source of new sacred texts and secret sciences given through the prism of all Seven Rays, just like that "one small parent volume"[42] whose stanzas Blavatsky presented in *The Secret Doctrine* — a work which has crowned everything that has ever been given for current humanity and has paved its path into the future.

The Age of the *Book of Dzyan*

Now as to the age of the *Book of Dzyan*, it is actually impossible to determine, because it is a living Book that continues its development and evolution together with humanity. On the one hand, its secret folios may turn out to be even more ancient than our planet, while on the other hand, its newest volumes are only about 5000 years old, and give us an assurance that this sacred work has not yet been finished.

However, the volumes of the *Book of Dzyan* should not be considered in isolation from each other. Indeed, they all represent branches with their own components, or offshoots, reared on the unified Tree of Life and nourished by the roots of the One Source.

For this reason, no matter what timepoint we select to describe this secret manuscript of untold antiquity — 300

million, 5 million, 1 million, or a few thousand years —
everything will be correct and will not contradict Truth.
Of course, the version that it is nearly one million years
old has become the most widespread, thanks to Helena
Blavatsky, who was the first to tell the modern world
about the existence of the *Book of Dzyan*.

The Language of the *Book of Dzyan*

Like all secret manuscripts stored in Shambhala, the
Book of Dzyan is written in the sacred language of
Senzar. It is the "materialized form" of the Voice of the
Silence in which everything speaks in the Universe, and
which every enlightened human heart is capable of un-
derstanding.

At the basis of the *Senzar* language lies a symbolism
closely associated with sound, colour, light, and number.
Formerly, this language was available to all humanity, but
now only the Masters and Their disciples speak it.

The language of *Senzar* consists of many levels. Its
highest manifestations are the closest to the Voice of the
Silence, which include thought-forms, the breathing of
fires, the geometric expression from combinations of rays,
and so on — these are simply impossible to explain in any
human tongue — whereas its lowest manifestations re-
semble traditional writing systems with their own specific
rules. Thus, the Angelic language of John Dee, a mysterious advisor to Queen Elizabeth I, is *one of the variants* of
the script in the *Senzar* language.

The Symbolism of the *Book of Dzyan*

In *The Secret Doctrine* Helena Blavatsky described some pages of the *Book of Dzyan* as follows: "On the first page is an immaculate white disk within a dull black ground"; "On the following page, the same disk, but with a central point."[43]

The immaculate white Disc in the given context suggests a certain new Cycle, a Round for the manifestation of the Fire that, according to the Supreme Will (Plan), is foreordained for precipitation on a particular soil. This soil will develop the ability to absorb a high-frequency substance that will launch a chain of alchemical reactions. The black ground here signifies the unmanifested Wisdom of the Cosmos, or a field (the Earth, as well as any other cosmic "bodies" connected with the planet) whereon the Great Sowing must be made.

On the esoteric plane, the Point in the Disc symbolizes the first unmanifested Logos that is called upon to emerge over the infinite extent of Space and Time represented by the Round. Then the Point turns into a diameter, starting to unfold on a certain Plane of Absoluteness and Infinity, giving rise to a further chain of "geometrical figures."

All the symbols mentioned above have countless numbers of hidden meanings; these emerge one from another, and are the most significant geometrical figures from the viewpoint of metaphysics. For example, John the Baptist and John the Evangelist, in one of the sacred meanings in relation to the Point, are the two vertical parallels accompanying the Point. They also represent an example of fulfilling one's duty to both humanity and God (within the limits of the outlined Round).

Thus, it is possible to reflect upon just a single page of the *Book of Dzyan* for years, endlessly unfolding the meanings of the symbols presented on it. And the correctness of disciples' understanding depends on their intuition, which in turn is based on the energies accumulated throughout many lifetimes within their hearts — in the form of a crystal known as *Ringsel* in Tibet. Hence another meaning of the word *Dzyan* as a derivative of the Sanskrit *Dhyan*: attaining wisdom through meditation or contemplation.

Methods for Transmitting Excerpts from Secret Manuscripts

Unlike a fragment of the Chintamani Stone, the *Book of Dzyan* in its natural form cannot be placed in someone's hands, but through the efforts of a Teacher abiding in the Stronghold of Light, some of its pages which the Master holds in His gaze can be "imprinted" on space. And, before the eyes of His disciple, a text begins to emerge which may take the form of characters of various colours and sizes, as well as of stable or "breathing" geometric shapes, and so on. Of course, only one who possesses inner clairvoyance and has properly developed the ability to see through the eye of the heart, can penetrate the depth of the text.

It is not necessary for the disciples who are destined to reveal any part of the *Book of Dzyan* to visit Shambhala in their physical bodies — an excerpt can be transmitted directly from Master to disciple. So, Helena Blavatsky was called to Shambhala and saw this manuscript with her own eyes, but *Theogenesis* was received by Francia La Due from the Master Hilarion.

A similar example is known with another secret manuscript entitled the *Book of the Golden Precepts* that is stored in the Tower of Chung as well. Blavatsky published three excerpts from it in her book *The Voice of the Silence*, which was later endorsed by the 9th Panchen Lama and the 14th Dalai Lama. However, during her lifetime, and she herself confirmed this,[44] another excerpt entitled *Light on the Path* was revealed through Mabel Collins. As became known later, it was given by the Master Hilarion.[45]

Guardians of Stanzas from the *Book of Dzyan*

At the moment not everything related to the work of the Masters on sacral texts is allowed to be disclosed. However, it can be said that each already published excerpt from the volumes of the *Book of Dzyan* had its own Guardian.

As already mentioned, all Supreme Lords have access to the secret pages of the *Book of Dzyan*. Moreover, They are permitted to copy any excerpt from the sacred texts. This is in accord with the decision of the Council of Shambhala — made on the basis of the Law of Expediency, which dictates the need to reveal yet another page of Secret Knowledge to the world.

Each of the Seven Teachers supervises a particular continent. And already in these lands certain cosmic and space conditions are formed, indicating that the "soil" is ready for the Sowing. Until then, the Lord who is the Protector of a certain continent, or a part of the world, is the Guardian of particular stanzas from the volumes of the *Book of Dzyan*.

So the Guardian of the stanzas of *Cosmogenesis* and *Anthropogenesis* was the Master Morya, who oversees the

Slavic and Indian lands and neighbouring soils, as well as the islands of Great Britain and Japan, which are connected with the future.

The Master Rákóczi, also known as Count Saint-Germain, was the Guardian of the stanzas of *Theogenesis* at that time. Under His auspices are Europe and North America. But the latter is also under the patronage of the Master Hilarion, and therefore, it is quite logical that, in His co-operation with Francia La Due, the above-mentioned excerpt was given by the Lord Saint-Germain, with whom They work together on this continent.

As for the stanzas of *Agapegenesis*, their Guardian, too, was the Master Morya who, with the advent of the Age of Aquarius, took the Name of Maitreya — the Lord of Love and Compassion. Therefore, this excerpt could have been given solely through the Ray of Love-Wisdom.

The Uniqueness of the Excerpts from the *Book of Dzyan*

Each revealed excerpt from the *Book of Dzyan* is unique and inimitable. It cannot be compared with any previous excerpt, or be expected to precisely reproduce its style or content, since these were given at different times and for different purposes. The Space-Time continuums have undergone a multitude of changes since then, which eventually had an effect on humanity as well. Each epoch, calculated in terms of a 60-year cycle, has its own unique rhythm of sound at the level of energy components.

Thus, under the Law of Expediency, only the Supreme Masters are entitled to determine the rhythm, style, content, and energy components of any Secret Knowledge to be revealed to humanity. Through which Ray and through whom to convey the lines impressed upon the pages of sacral texts — such decisions, again, fall only within the competence of the Great Lords, who have insight into the totality of the patterns connecting the planet Earth and the whole Solar System with other planets and constellations.

The human gaze can glimpse only the surface of the soil in whose depths a seed has been planted. To see what kind of a shoot will break through and what will eventually grow out of it — not to mention what fruit it will yield — this requires time. And it goes without saying that only the eye of the heart is able to behold the final harvest to be reaped by the Great Sower at the end of Times.

The Sacred Significance of the *Book of Dzyan*

The *Book of Dzyan* reveals itself gradually, depending on the tasks set before the totality of the Brotherhood's colleagues. So, readers who hold in their hands a published book in which are embedded some of the lines of the *Book of Dzyan*, may not fully understand its text. Yet the energy contained in the book is already affecting them on a cellular level, helping them rise to the next cycle of Evolution. Not only that, but this effect is increased thanks to the emanations of the Chintamani Stone. These emanations are "interwoven" into a single life-affirming pattern with the purpose of creating a human being who is not only rational, but also wise — and wisdom, as we know, may be found only where hearts are brimming over with Love.

Appendix

Additional Explanations of Helena Blavatsky's Statement about 1975

In her instructions for students of the Esoteric Section, Helena Blavatsky wrote about the opportunity "given to the world in every last quarter of a century,"[46] mentioning the year 1975. But in the following paragraphs, she also said that the student was required to use all his powers in examining what was given, "so that the inner meaning of the instructions may be impressed upon him apart from the words in which they are clothed."[47]

In addition, one should draw attention to the following words Blavatsky included in the same instructions: "And if her place is even filled up, perchance by another worthier and more learned than herself, still there remain but twelve years to the last hour of the term — namely, till December the 31st, 1899."[48]

Helena Roerich's birthday was on 31 January (12 February)* 1879, and here the following points should be noted:

---

* The twelve-day difference here is due to the use of the old Julian calendar still prevalent in Russia before 1918.

1. The symbolism of the number should be viewed as 31 January 1879 — this date will also be different numerologically.

2. In the East, one's birthday is considered as the day of conception ("the seed was thrown into the soil," i.e., when the materialization of one's physical form begins). Deducting nine months, we get an approximate date of the end of April or the beginning of May 1878. Of course, the day and hour marked with the beginning of unfolding life at the level of the first cell division, is considered a sacrament, and is known only to the Teacher who, according to the Supreme Plan, guided His future disciple from the Subtle World into the physical.

3. From the first days of the development of the embryo, a phased work occurs, and, now by the age of 12, the spirit of the disciple is ready to manifest upon his subtle structures, including the mental body, a superimposed matrix. This matrix represents a number of tasks set by the Supreme Powers that the disciple is to accomplish in subsequent years. And so, by May 1890, in addition to establishing her own energy sound, Helena Roerich also accepted a part of the vital currents which, through the method of "flowing fires," were "separated" from Helena Blavatsky, who was still in her physical body.

4. The spirit of succession is established not only between the Master and His disciple, but also takes place between those disciples on whose shoulders is laid the mission to solve certain tasks assigned by the Teachers of humanity. In this way, regardless of time and space, the fires gained by one disciple may partially flow into another, and so on.

5. And if we speak about "another worthier and more learned than herself, still there remain but twelve years to the last hour of the term — namely, till December the

31st, 1899," then we can assert with confidence that Helena Roerich appeared just at the right time.

Of course, only a part of the Lord's Plan was disclosed to Helena Blavatsky, since it is difficult for the human gaze to embrace the entire spectrum of the Cosmic Pattern. And it is accessible only to Those who stand at the Helm of Evolution, every day and hour introducing stellar adjustments to the Plan, after taking emerging cosmic and spatial conditions into account.

From the notebooks of Helena Roerich, in which she recorded her conversations with the Master Morya, it is known that while Blavatsky at that time could not speak about the periods in writing, she did impart them to her closest colleagues verbally.[49]

However, this entrusted information was misinterpreted: instead of waiting for a new disciple, as mentioned by Blavatsky herself,[50] there arose an anticipation of a "World Teacher" in a physical body. Yet it is still interesting to note that this "anticipation" was scheduled not in 1975–2000, as Blavatsky stated in writing, but in the 1920–1930s that coincided with the completion of the next 60-year cycle. This suggests that Blavatsky did convey to her closest colleagues that the following disciple must be sent by the Masters much earlier than the date she was permitted to mention publicly.

As for the statement that, "No Master of Wisdom from the East will himself appear or send anyone to Europe or America after that period, . . . until the year 1975,"[51] here, apart from the symbolism implying the Oriental sexagenary cycles, the following was also meant.

At the end of the 19th century, all the Secret Schools were closed, because at the threshold of two world wars, the atmosphere became so poisoned and unbearable that the Masters could no longer stay among people. Ashrams were closed not only in Egypt and Europe, but even in Tibet (for example, in Shigatse). All the Teachers who worked with disciples were summoned to the Chief Stronghold in the Himalayas. This was also connected with the forthcoming date of 1936; Blavatsky knew for sure about this date and told her companions verbally.

Furthermore, Edgar Cayce was asked about the calculations found in the Great Pyramid by researchers David Davidson and Herbert Aldersmith and published in their book *The Great Pyramid: Its Divine Message*. They pointed to the importance of the year 1936 in human history. Cayce confirmed the correctness of many of their conclusions, but also indicated that, "Only an initiate may understand."[52]

From all the above, it does not follow that Blavatsky was "wrong" or "led someone into error" when she talked about the last quarter of each century. She simply did not specify that this was related to the Brotherhood of Luxor in Thebes, Egypt, whose mission has always been to lead the peoples of the West through the mind to the heart, and naturally it followed the 100-year cycles.

In the past, it was the Masters and disciples of the Theban Sanctuary that often incarnated themselves within the specified periods. However, Mahatmas Morya and Koot Hoomi who guided Blavatsky have always been representatives of the Himalayan Brotherhood, which has lived according to the 60-year epochs. Blavatsky herself belonged to the Western Lodge, yet subsequently she became a representative of the Eastern Lodge of the White Brotherhood.

If we observe the history of scientific discoveries, we can note certain numbers and rhythms. And, of course, many spirits who brought discoveries to the world in various domains of science have started to incarnate themselves since 1975 — some even earlier, depending on which celestial orb they needed to come under. After all, it is in this period that the foundation was laid for the leap in technological progress that we see today. And do not the disciples of the Theban Sanctuary stand behind all this?

But what else should be borne in mind is that the Lords may manifest Themselves in the subtle bodies of a special rarefied structure in any century. And, of course, the energy formula of the body of Mahatma M. during Blavatsky's time will be significantly different from the one in which it appeared to the gaze of Helena Roerich.

The physical flesh of the Lord as seen by Blavatsky, of course, can never be beheld by any future disciple. This is because His body, after accomplishing a specific mission, undergoes a process of alchemical transfiguration, which is akin to the "burning" of those sound constants of currents typical for the rhythm of the previous century, although the body of the Lord surpassed it in its basic fiery currents.

In order to help the space defined by the particular boundaries of Time, it is necessary for one of the densified bodies of the Lord to attune itself to the rhythm of the century, with the aim of accomplishing Cosmic Tasks more successfully — and then, on the basis of the currents established in the world, to introduce new fiery ingredients that will allow for the composition of a new cycle of Evolution.

Then, when the majority of the rhythms of the previous century become obsolete, they will not impede new constructions of Cosmic Patterns. And then the subtle structure of the Lord is composed in a higher constant of sound. Later, to the disciple connected with Him, an Image may be revealed which the Lord considers appropriate to manifest either before the eye of the heart or through the so-called "third eye" of the disciple.

High Spirits will never burden Their subtle bodies with obsolete currents, but every moment They will bring into the world new Fires — and these also contribute to the rearrangement of Their bodies, according to the Behest of Time, as well as of Timelessness.

Notes

1. Helena Blavatsky, *The Secret Doctrine*, vol. 1 (London: Theosophical Publishing Company, 1888), p. xliii.

2. See Blavatsky, *The Secret Doctrine*, vol. 1, pp. xxxvii–xxxviii, xlv.

3. See *The Mahatma Letters to A.P. Sinnett*, comp. Trevor Baker (Pasadena, CA: Theosophical University Press, 1992), p. 362.

4. See Georges de Roerich, "Studies in the Kalacakra," *Journal of the 'Urusvati' Himalayan Research Institute of the Roerich Museum*, vol. 2 (1932), pp. 11–23; Helena Blavatsky, "Secret Cycles," *Collected Writings*, vol. 14 (Wheaton, IL: Theosophical Publishing House, 1966), pp. 359–360.

5. Helena Blavatsky, *The Key to Theosophy* (London: The Theosophical Publishing Company, 1889), p. 306.

6. Blavatsky, "Tsong-Kha-Pa — Lohans in China," *Collected Writings*, vol. 14, p. 431.

7. See Blavatsky, *The Key to Theosophy*, pp. 306–307.

8. Blavatsky, *The Secret Doctrine*, vol. 1, p. xxxviii.

9. Helena Blavatsky, "The Esoteric Character of the Gospels," *Collected Writings*, vol. 8 (Wheaton, IL: Theosophical Publishing House, 1966), p. 205.

10. See Helena Roerich, *Pis'ma*, vol. 9 (Moscow: Mezhdunarodnyi tsentr Rerikhov, 2009), pp. 415, 439.

11. Helena Roerich, *Fiery World*, vol. 1 (New York: Agni Yoga Society, 1969), pp. 312, 320.

12. Associated Press, "Climate change is behind the 'weirdness' of Earth's current weather as 118 of all-time heat records have been set or tied across the globe," *Daily Mail Online*, http://www.dailymail.co.uk/sciencetech/article-6000715/Science-says-record-heat-fires-worsened-climate-change.html.

13. Chris Mooney, "The next five years will be 'anomalously warm,' scientists predict," *The Washington Post*, https://www.washingtonpost.com/energy-environment/2018/08/14/next-five-years-will-be-anomalously-warm-scientists-predict.

14. Nigel Henbest and Heather Couper, *The Guide to the Galaxy* (Cambridge: Cambridge University Press, 1994), p. 93.

15. Helena Roerich, "Zapisi besed s Uchitelem (iogicheskie praktiki)," 1953, fol. 62, Roerich Museum, Moscow.

16. World Health Organization, "Cardiovascular diseases (CVDs)," http://www.who.int/news-room/fact-sheets/detail/cardiovascular-diseases-(cvds).

17. See Helena Blavatsky, "Esoteric Instructions," *Collected Writings*, vol. 12 (Wheaton, IL: Theosophical Publishing House, 1980), pp. 694–695.

18. Helena Blavatsky, *The Voice of the Silence* (London: The Theosophical Publishing Company, 1889), p. 27.

19. "Voyager Experiences Three 'Tsunami Waves' in Interstellar Space," *Jet Propulsion Laboratory*, https://www.jpl.nasa.gov/video/details.php?id=1347; "Sun Sends More 'Tsunami Waves' to Voyager 1," *Jet Propulsion*

Laboratory, https://voyager.jpl.nasa.gov/news/details. php?article_id=38; "NASA Voyager: 'Tsunami Wave' Still Flies Through Interstellar Space," *Jet Propulsion Laboratory*, https://www.jpl.nasa.gov/news/news.php? feature=4411.

20. Deborah Netburn, "In human cells, scientists find DNA that looks like a twisted knot instead of a double helix," *Los Angeles Times*, https://www.latimes.com/ science/sciencenow/la-sci-sn-dna-i-motif-20180423-story.html.

21. "Worldwide cancer cases expected to soar by 70% over next 20 years," *The Guardian*, https://www. theguardian.com/society/2014/feb/03/worldwide-cancer-cases-soar-next-20-years.

22. See Blavatsky, *The Secret Doctrine*, vol. 1, p. xliv.

23. See *ibid.*, pp. 170, 206.

24. See Helena Roerich, *Zapisi Ucheniia Zhivoi Etiki*, vol. 8 (Moscow, 2010), p. 414.

25. See Blavatsky, *The Secret Doctrine*, vol. 1, p. 378.

26. Aleksei Popov, *Kareliia neizvestnaia* (Petroza-vodsk: Raseia, 2010), p. 163.

27. *Ibid.*, p. 165.

28. *Ibid.*, p. 170.

29. See Blavatsky, *The Secret Doctrine*, vol. 2, p. 6.

30. Edgar Cayce, *The Complete Edgar Cayce Readings* (Virginia Beach, VA: A.R.E. Press, 2006), CD-ROM, Reading 5748–6.

31. "Responses to Your Questions," *NOVA Online Adventure*, https://www.pbs.org/wgbh/nova/pyramid/ mail/responses970210.html.

32. Incorporated Society for Psychical Research, "Madame Blavatsky, co-founder of the Theosophical Society, was unjustly condemned, new study concludes," press release, 8 May 1986.

33. Joseph H. Fussell, *Incidents in the History of the Theosophical Movement* (Point Loma, CA: Aryan Theosophical Press, 1920), p. 7.

34. Nicholas Roerich, *Altai-Himalaya: A Travel Diary* (New York: Frederick A. Stokes Company, 1929), pp. 125–126.

35. Bhairab Chaitanya, *Swami Abhedananda's Journey into Kashmir and Tibet* (Calcutta: Ramakrishna Vedanta Math, 1987), pp. 119–121.

36. Helena Roerich, "Zapisi besed s Uchitelem (mashinopis')," 1952–1954, part 1, fol. 52, Roerich Museum, Moscow.

37. *Ibid.*, fols. 74–75.

38. *Ibid.*, fol. 52.

39. See Blavatsky, *The Secret Doctrine*, vol. 1, p. 1.

40. See Blavatsky, "The Secret Books of Lam-Rim and Dzyan," *Collected Writings*, vol. 14, p. 422.

41. See Blavatsky, *The Secret Doctrine*, vol. 1, p. xliii.

42. *Ibid.*

43. Blavatsky, *The Secret Doctrine*, vol. 1, p. 1.

44. Helena Blavatsky, "Literary Jottings," *Lucifer: A Theosophical Magazine*, vol. 3 (September 1888–February 1889), p. 347.

45. Francia La Due, *Teachings of the Temple*, vol. 2 (Halcyon, CA: Temple of the People, 1985), p. 4.

46. See Blavatsky, "Esoteric Instructions," *Collected Writings*, vol. 12, p. 492.

47. *Ibid.*, p. 493.

48. *Ibid.*, pp. 491–492.

49. See Helena Roerich, *Zapisi Ucheniia Zhivoi Etiki*, vol. 15 (Wismar-Vologda, 2012), p. 208.

50. See Blavatsky, *The Key to Theosophy*, pp. 306–307.

51. Blavatsky, "Esoteric Instructions," *Collected Writings*, vol. 12, p. 492.

52. Cayce, *The Complete Edgar Cayce Readings*, Reading 5748–5.

About the Author

 **Zinovia Vasilievna Dushkova**, Ph.D., is a Russian author, poet, philosopher, historian, and traveller. She has been honoured with a number of awards, prizes, and commendations for her contribution to the spiritual development of society and for merit in the domain of scientific research in the ecology of consciousness. She is a Fellow of the European Academy of Natural Sciences and the European Scientific Society, both based in Hanover, Germany.

Dr. Dushkova's interest in the history of world religions and philosophy, along with a desire to realize and fulfil her mission in life, led her first to the wisdom of prominent philosophers and thinkers, and subsequently to the works of Helena Blavatsky and the Roerichs, which changed her life radically. It is said in Oriental teachings that when the disciple is ready, the Teacher will appear — thus, in 1992, the Master came to her. After three years of intense training and probation, in 1995 she embarked on her first trip to India — the land of ancient teachings. There, at the foot of the sacred Himalayas, in the Buddhist

Ghoom Monastery — where Madame Blavatsky in 1882 and Helena Roerich in 1923 met with the Master M. — the path of Zinovia Dushkova began.

The mysterious paths — leading into the heart of the Himalayas and the Blue Mountains, in the vicinity of Mounts Kanchenjunga, Kailash, Everest, and so on — brought Dushkova to the secret Abodes of Light, from where the Call had sounded. Much like a hermit monk, she started poring over the sacred manuscripts that had been preserved in the most hidden corners of Sikkim, Ladakh, and other unexplored places of India. Thus, she gained admittance to the secret *Book of Dzyan*, the stanzas of which were first revealed by Helena Blavatsky, forming the basis of *The Secret Doctrine*. A new excerpt from this mysterious manuscript was later published in *The Book of Secret Wisdom*.

Dr. Dushkova has devoted more than 25 years of her life to the study and acquisition of hidden esoteric wisdom, which she is now sharing with people through her books. She is the author of approximately forty works, published in Russia, Ukraine, Moldova, and France. These works of an ethical and spiritual nature reflect a synthesis of science, religion, history, and philosophy. Underlying her poetry and prose, fairy tales and legends, is a worldview full of wisdom and the cultural heritage of both the East and the West.

Zinovia Dushkova's major works, *The Teaching of the Heart*, *The Fiery Bible*, and *The Secret Doctrine of Love*, have called forth a wave of social movement in Russia, Ukraine, and Kazakhstan, centred around the development of culture, science, and education, all of which contribute to the progress and prosperity of society. Her award-winning philosophical children's book, *Fairy Tales for the Saviour*, has been given a ringing endorsement by teachers working with problem children in orphanages and juvenile detention centres.

Reigniting hope where it has disappeared, illuminating love where it has died away, and adding delight to life where its meaning has been lost — this is the goal which Dr. Zinovia Dushkova strives to attain in all her writings.

Visit the author's official website at:

www.dushkova.com/en/

Sign up for the author's newsletter at:

www.dushkova.com/en/sign-up

Follow the author at:

www.facebook.com/ZinoviaDushkova

www.twitter.com/ZinoviaDushkova

www.goodreads.com/ZinoviaDushkova

Also by the Author

The Book of Secret Wisdom

Do you wonder about the future and the destiny of humanity? Do you want to know the true purpose of your existence on Earth and in the Universe? A long-hidden ancient text holds the answers you seek!

Zinovia Dushkova, Ph.D., is one of the few living people who has gained access to the million-year-old manuscript widely known as the *Book of Dzyan*. Written in the language of the Gods, called *Senzar*, it is secretly hidden in the heart of the Himalayas, accessible to only a chosen few over the course of human history, including Gautama Buddha, Jesus Christ, Pythagoras, Plato, and Helena Blavatsky. Interpretations of various parts of this secret manuscript, presented in different lights, can be found in all religions and philosophies.

Now, for the first time ever, Dr. Dushkova has presented a never-before-seen excerpt from this ancient sacred text in *The Book of Secret Wisdom*. Beautiful and enlightening, it will reveal not only our past, but also our present and future. To facilitate your understanding of this profound and poetic text, the book contains a comprehensive glossary gleaned from the supreme sources of wisdom.

In *The Book of Secret Wisdom*, you will discover the answers to these questions:

- What are the ultimate goal and purpose of human existence?
- What is the cause of destructive weather, natural disasters, and global warming?
- What really happened in 1999 and 2012?
- What Great Event occurred invisibly in 2017?
- What should you expect in the coming decades?
- When did Armageddon and the Last Judgment occur?
- Why are people dying, and is there a chance to be immortal?
- Why does it seem that time is speeding up?
- What is the famous Philosopher's Stone?
- and much, *much* more!

The all-embracing and undistorted Truth presented in this book was once accessible only to the privileged initiates of ancient civilizations who spent much of their lives seeking it. But now it is available to you in the pages of *The Book of Secret Wisdom*, a book that offers unprecedented access to the world's most ancient mysteries.

If you are a spiritual seeker who enjoys expanding the boundaries of your understanding, this book is for you.

Get *The Book of Secret Wisdom* now to unveil the world's most ancient mysteries!

The Teaching of the Heart

For the first time in history, the Masters of Wisdom have opened their treasury of secret knowledge to reveal the highest Teaching. This Teaching will empower you to transform yourself and the world through awakening the omnipotent power hidden in your heart.

Existing since time immemorial and called *Surya-Vidya* in antiquity, this Teaching taught the most worthy people about the sacred meaning of the heart as the sun of their universe — an inexhaustible source of perfect wisdom and divine power. However, humanity was not ready to accept the prevailing role of the heart. Therefore, the Teaching of the Heart has been kept secret and remained the prerogative of only the chosen few — those spiritual teachers who have proclaimed the omnipotence of the pure and loving heart.

The time has come to awaken humanity to the almighty treasure we possess because its infinite possibilities can radically change not only individual lives, but also the entire suffering world for the better. This mission has been undertaken by the Greatest Teacher known as the *Great Heart* — the Lord of Love and Compassion, the King of the legendary kingdom of Shambhala hidden in the Himalayas. He is Maitreya for some, Christ for others, and the Mahdi for many more — He is the promised Messiah of all religions. Before coming into the world, He has given *The Teaching of the Heart*, making it accessible to everyone for daily use in modern life.

Employing a *spiral approach*, the inspirational and uplifting books of *The Teaching of the Heart* series will reveal your heart's secret powers and cover a wide range of topics from everyday life to travels within the Universe.

The Teaching of the Heart was written by Zinovia Du-shkova, Ph.D., through a unique creative process called the *Fiery Experience*. She continues the spiritual tradition of the hidden Himalayan Masters who guided Helena Blavatsky and Helena Roerich to lead humanity from intellectual knowledge to the divine wisdom of the heart.

If you would like a wise Teacher to guide you through life, offer uplifting advice, and help you fulfil your spiritual potential and true purpose, this book series is for you.

Embark on a fascinating spiritual journey with the Greatest Master of Wisdom today to awaken the power of your heart!

Parables from Shambhala

This inspirational little book will help you comprehend the greatest ancient truths of the East through twelve short and profound parables containing the universal Laws of Existence. These truths will be revealed to you through the juxtaposition of opposites: spirit and body, reality and illusion, good and evil, freedom and slavery, life and death, and so on. In this way, the spiritual lessons of this wonderful book will enable you to make the right decisions in your daily life and to respond with wisdom to the events happening around you.

These parables were left as a heritage to humanity by the Mahatmas, the Great Souls of the East, and written down by Zinovia Dushkova, Ph.D., an award-winning author. During her trips across Tibet, India, Nepal, and Mongolia, she has stayed at numerous monasteries — those open to the public as well as those hidden within high mountains and caves. She has been honoured to communicate with representatives of different religions, elderly monks and hermits who have generously shared their secret knowledge with her. In 2004, one Himalayan Master of Wisdom narrated legends and tales originating from the mysterious kingdom of Shambhala. This experience inspired the author to write down the stories in this book of parables under the canopy of the gigantic deodar cedars on the summit of the Himalayas.

Parables from Shambhala will be your loyal companion during your journey of self-improvement and spiritual growth, revealing its symbolism and depth as your consciousness expands.